## Acclaim for *In Praise of Love*

"[Badiou] leaves the reader with an incisive overview of philosophical thinking on love, from Plato to Kierkegaard to Lacan. . . . The struggle to understand such a mystifying phenomenon invariably requires the help of philosophers. . . . Good news for Mr. Badiou."
                                                    —*The Economist*

"Finally, the cure for the pornographic, utilitarian exchange of favors to which love has been reduced in America. Alain Badiou is our philosopher of love."
                    —Simon Critchley, Hans Jonas Professor
                        at The New School for Social Research
                        and author of *The Faith of the Faithless*

"Elegant and deeply human, *In Praise of Love* is a conversational but erudite retort to the antiseptic promises of online dating sites for 'safe love' without risk, the romantic notion that love is the ecstatic melding of two into one, and the philosophical skepticism that love is little more than a cover story for sexual lust."

                        —Pamela Haag, PhD, author of *Marriage
                        Confidential: Love in the Post-Romantic Age*
                        and columnist at *Big Think*

# Acclaim for Alain Badiou

"A figure like Plato or Hegel walks here among us!"
—Slavoj Žižek

"An heir to Jean-Paul Sartre and Louis Althusser."
—*New Statesman*

"Scarcely any other moral philosopher of our day is as politically clear-sighted and courageously polemical, so prepared to put notions of truth and universality back on the agenda."
—Terry Eagleton

Born in Rabat, Morocco, in 1937, **Alain Badiou** is a leading French philosopher. A lifelong communist, he is the author of *The Meaning of Sarkozy*, *Being and Event*, *Ethics: An Essay on the Understanding of Evil*, and *The Communist Hypothesis*. He lives in Paris. **Nicolas Truong** is a writer, journalist, and regular contributor to the French daily *Le Monde*. **Peter Bush** is an award-winning literary translator. He lives in Barcelona.

# IN PRAISE *of* LOVE

## ALAIN BADIOU

with Nicolas Truong

*Translated by Peter Bush*

The New Press gratefully acknowledges the Florence Gould
Foundation for supporting publication of this book.

Originally published in France as *Éloge de l'amour*
by Flammarion SA, Paris, 2009
Published in the United Kingdom by Serpent's Tail, London, 2012
Published in the United States by The New Press, New York, 2012
Distributed by Perseus Distribution

CIP data is available
ISBN 978-1-59558-877-7 (hc.)

The New Press publishes books that promote and enrich
public discussion and understanding of the issues vital to our
democracy and to a more equitable world. These books are made
possible by the enthusiasm of our readers; the support of a
committed group of donors, large and small; the collaboration
of our many partners in the independent media and the
not-for-profit sector; booksellers, who often hand-sell
New Press books; librarians; and above all by our authors.

www.thenewpress.com

Printed in the United States of America

2 4 6 8 10 9 7 5 3 1

"As we know, love needs re-inventing."

Arthur Rimbaud
*A season in hell, Hallucinations 1*

# CONTENTS

# INTRODUCTION

A philosopher must never forget the countless situations in life when he is no different from anyone else. If he does, theatrical tradition, particularly comedy, will rudely remind him of that fact. There is, after all, a stock stage character, the philosopher in love, whose Stoic wisdom and well-rehearsed distrust of passion evaporate in their entirety the moment a dazzlingly beautiful woman sweeps into the room and blows him away forever.

I realised this a long time ago. I have suggested that a philosopher (and this neutral noun naturally encompasses both male and female varieties) must be an accomplished scientist, an amateur poet and a political activist, but also has to accept that the realm of thought is never sealed off from the violent onslaughts of love. Philosophy requires its practitioners of either gender to assume the roles of savant, artist, activist and lover. I have called them the four *conditions* of philosophy.

That was why I immediately agreed when Nicolas Truong invited me to join him in conversation in the "Theatre of Ideas" series he organises at the Avignon Festival. It looked as if it would be a delicious cocktail of theatre, crowds, conversation, love and philosophy. Besides, it was going to be held on 14 July (2008) and I was excited by the idea of celebrating love, a cosmopolitan, subversive, sexual energy that transgresses frontiers and social status at a time normally devoted to the Army, the Nation and the State.

Let's now blow our own trumpet a little:

# IN PRAISE OF LOVE

❧

Nicolas asked the questions, and I performed the ambiguous role of a philosopher of love, we worked well together and it was a success. No doubt about it: it was a hit.

The text you are about to read is an elaboration of what we said on the day. It retains the spontaneous rhythm, clarity and energy but is more rounded and incisive. I believe that, from start to finish, it is what it says it is: praise of love, sung by a philosopher who thinks, like Plato, whom I quote: "Anyone who doesn't take love as a starting point will never understand the nature of philosophy". So here you have Alain Badiou, the philosopher lover, tussling with Nicolas Truong, a wise interrogator, a philosopher, and, of course, a lover.

# I

# LOVE UNDER THREAT

*In* The Meaning of Sarkozy, *a book that has subsequently become famous, you argue that "we must re-invent love but also quite simply defend it, because it faces threats from all sides". In what ways is it threatened? How, in your view, have the arranged marriages of yesteryear been re-packaged in the new clothes of today? I believe that recent publicity for a dating website has particularly struck you...*

That's right, Paris is plastered with posters for the Meetic internet dating-site, whose ads I find really disturbing. I could mention a number of slogans its hype uses. The first misappropriates the title of Marivaux's play, *The Game of Love and Chance*, "Get love without chance!" And then another says: "Be in love without falling in love!" No raptures, right? Then: "Get perfect love without suffering!" And all thanks to the Meetic dating-site... that offers into the bargain – and the notion takes my breath away – "coaching in love". So they supply you with a trainer who will prepare you to face the test.

I believe this hype reflects a safety-first concept of "love". It is love comprehensively insured against all risks: you will have love, but will have assessed the prospective relationship so thoroughly, will have selected your partner so carefully by searching online – by obtaining, of course, a photo, details of his or her tastes, date of birth, horoscope sign, etc. – and putting it all in the mix you can tell yourself: "This is a risk-free option!" That's their pitch and it's fascinating that the ad campaign should adopt it. Clearly, inasmuch as love is a pleasure almost everyone is looking for, the thing that gives meaning and intensity to almost everyone's life, I am convinced that love cannot be a gift given on the basis of a complete lack of risk. The Meetic approach reminds me of the propaganda of the American army when promoting the idea of "smart" bombs and "zero dead " wars.

*So do you think there is a connection between "zero dead" wars and "zero risk" love, in the same way that sociologists, Richard Sennett and Zygmunt Bauman, see an analogy between the "No commitment to you" that finance capitalism tells the casual worker to the "No commitment for my part" the "lover" tells his or her partner as they float in a world where relationships are made and unmade in the name of a cosy, consumerist permissiveness?*

It's all rather the same scenario. "Zero deaths" war, "zero risks" love, nothing random, no chance encounters. Backed as it is, with all the resources of a wide-scale advertising campaign, I see it as the first threat to love, what I would call the safety threat. After all, it's not so very different to an arranged marriage. Not done in the name of family order and hierarchy by despotic parents, but in the name of safety for the individuals involved, through advance agreements that avoid randomness, chance encounters and in the end any existential poetry, due to the categorical absence of risks.

The second threat love faces is to deny that it is at all important. The counterpoint to the safety threat is the idea that love is only a variant of rampant hedonism and the wide range of possible enjoyment. The aim is to avoid any immediate challenge, any deep and genuine experience of the otherness from which love is woven. However, we should add that as the risk factor can never be completely eliminated, Meetic's publicity, like the propaganda for imperial armies, says that the risks will be everyone else's! If you have been well trained for love, following the canons of modern safety, you won't find it difficult to dispatch the other person if they do not suit. If he suffers, that's his problem, right? He's not part of modernity. In the same way that "zero deaths" apply only to the Western military. The bombs they drop kill a lot of people who are to blame for living underneath. But these casualties are Afghans, Palestinians... They don't belong to modernity either. Safety-first love, like everything governed by the norm of safety, implies the absence of risks for people who have a good insurance policy, a good army, a good police force, a good psychological take on personal hedonism, and all risks for those on the opposite side.

You must have noticed how we are always

being told that things are being dealt with "for your comfort and safety", from potholes in pavements to police patrols in the metro. Love confronts two enemies, essentially: safety guaranteed by an insurance policy and the comfort zone limited by regulated pleasures.

*So there is a kind of pact between libertarian and liberal ideas on love?*

In effect I think that liberals and libertarians converge around the idea that love is a futile risk. And that, on the one hand, you can have a kind of well-planned marriage pursued with all the delights of consummation and, on the other, fun sexual arrangements full of pleasure, if you disregard passion. Seen from this perspective, I really do think that love, in today's world, is caught in this bind, in this vicious circle and is consequently under threat. I think it is the task

# IN PRAISE OF LOVE

of philosophy, as well as other fields, to rally to its defence. And that probably means, as the poet Rimbaud said, that it also needs re-inventing. It cannot be a defensive action simply to maintain the status quo. The world is full of new developments and love must also be something that innovates. Risk and adventure must be re-invented against safety and comfort.

# II

# PHILOSOPHERS AND LOVE

*You borrow from Rimbaud the phrase "Love needs re-inventing" and draw on numerous poets and writers as you develop your own conception of love. But first we should perhaps ask questions of other philosophers. You have been impressed by the fact that so few have shown a serious interest in love, and when they have, you usually disagree with them. Why?*

The relationship between philosophers and love is certainly far from straightforward. Aude Lancelin and Marie Lemonnier's *Philosophers and Love from Socrates to Simone de Beauvoir* shows that very clearly. The book has added interest in that it combines an examination of the philosophers' thinking and their lives without dumbing down. In that sense, it is almost unprecedented. The book shows how philosophy oscillates between two extremes when it comes to love, even though there are also intermediate points of view. On the one hand, there is "anti-love" philosophy, Arthur Schopenhauer being the prime representative of that tendency. He is well known for writing that he will never forgive women for experiencing a passion for love, thus making it possible to perpetuate a human species that was in fact worthless! He is one extreme. At the other, you find philosophers who transform love into one of the highest levels of subjective experience. That is the case with Sören Kierkegaard, for example. For Kierkegaard there are three levels of existence. At the aesthetic level, the experience of love is one of vain seduction and repetition. The selfishness of pleasure and the very selfishness of that selfishness drive individuals on, the archetype being Mozart's Don Juan. At the ethical level, love is genuine and demonstrates its own seriousness. It is an eternal commitment, turned towards the absolute, something Kierkegaard himself experienced in his long courtship of the young Régine. The ethical level can lead the way to the highest level, the religious level, if the absolute value of the commitment is endorsed by marriage. Marriage is thus conceived not as a strengthening of the social bond against the perils of wayward love, but as the institution that channels genuine love towards its fundamental destination. The final transfiguration of love becomes possible when "the Ego plunges through its own transparency to meet the power that has created it": that is, when, thanks to the experience of love, the Ego roots itself in its divine source. Love then moves

❦

beyond seduction and, through the serious mediation of marriage, becomes a way to accede to the super-human.

As you can see, philosophy struggles with huge tension. On the one hand, love seen as a natural extravagance of sex arouses a kind of rational suspicion. Conversely, we see an apology for love that borders on religious epiphany. Christianity hovers in the background, a religion of love after all. And the tension is almost unbearable. Thus, when Kierkegaard was finally unable to contemplate the idea of marrying Régine, he broke with her. In the end, he represented the aesthete seducer of the first level, lived the ethical promise of the second and failed to make the transition, via the real-life seriousness of marriage, to the third level. Nonetheless, he visited the whole gamut of forms of philosophical reflection on love.

*Does your own interest in this question go back to
the initial move made by Plato who turns love into
one of the ways of approaching the Idea?*

Plato is quite precise in what he says about love:
a seed of universality resides in the impulse
towards love. The experience of love is an impulse
towards something that he calls the Idea. Thus,
even when I am merely admiring a beautiful
body, whether I like it or not, I am in movement
towards the idea of Beauty. I think – in quite
different terms, naturally – along the same lines,
namely that love encompasses the experience of
the possible transition from the pure randomness
of chance to a state that has universal value.
Starting out from something that is simply an
encounter, a trifle, you learn that you can experience the world on the basis of difference and
not only in terms of identity. And you can even
be tested and suffer in the process. In today's

world, it is generally thought that individuals only pursue their own self-interest. Love is an antidote to that. Provided it isn't conceived only as an exchange of mutual favours, or isn't calculated way in advance as a profitable investment, love really is a unique trust placed in chance. It takes us into key areas of the experience of what is difference and, essentially, leads to the idea that you can experience the world from the perspective of difference. In this respect it has universal implications: it is an individual experience of potential universality, and is thus central to philosophy, as Plato was the first to intuit.

*One of the great theorisers of love, according to you, Jacques Lacan, also engaged in dialogue with Plato and concluded, "there is no such thing as a sexual relationship". What did he mean?*

His is a very interesting thesis, derived from

a moralist, sceptical perspective, but one that leads to the contrary conclusion. Jacques Lacan reminds us, that in sex, each individual is to a large extent on their own, if I can put it that way. Naturally, the other's body has to be mediated, but at the end of the day, the pleasure will be always your pleasure. Sex separates, doesn't unite. The fact you are naked and pressing against the other is an image, an imaginary representation. What is real is that pleasure takes you a long way away, very far from the other. What is real is narcissistic, what binds is imaginary. So there is no such thing as a sexual relationship, concludes Lacan. His proposition shocked people since at the time everybody was talking about nothing else but "sexual relationships". If there is no sexual relationship in sexuality, love is what fills the absence of a sexual relationship.

Lacan doesn't say that love is a disguise for sexual relationships; he says that sexual

Narcissism = the pursuit of pleasure w/o the need or ability to fill the void w/ love.

relationships don't exist, that love is what comes to replace that non-relationship. That's much more interesting. This idea leads him to say that in love the other tries to approach "the being of the other". In love the individual goes beyond himself, beyond the narcissistic. In sex, you are really in a relationship with yourself via the mediation of the other. The other helps you to discover the reality of pleasure. In love, on the contrary, the mediation of the other is enough in itself. Such is the nature of the amorous encounter: you go to take on the other, to make him or her exist with you, as he or she is. It is a much more profound conception of love than the entirely banal view that love is no more than an imaginary canvas painted over the reality of sex.

In fact, Lacan also engages in philosophical ambiguities in relation to love. The idea that "love is what fills the absence of a sexual relationship" can indeed be interpreted in two ways.

The first and most obvious is that love is what the imagination employs to fill the emptiness created by sex. It is quite true, after all, that sex, however splendid it is and certainly can be, ends in a kind of emptiness. That is really why it is subject to the law of repetition: one must start time and time again. Every day, when one is young! Then love comes to be the idea that something exists in this void, that lovers are linked by something else apart from this relationship that doesn't exist.

When I was a very young man, I was very struck, almost disgusted, by a passage in Simone de Beauvoir's *The Second Sex*, where she describes, how, after having sex, the man feels the woman's body is flat and flabby and the woman feels in parallel that the man's body, apart from his erect member, is generally unattractive, if not slightly ridiculous. Theatrical farce or vaudeville makes us laugh with a constant usage of similar thoughts. Man's desire is the desire of the comic, big-bellied, impotent Phallus, and the toothless hag with sagging breasts is the future that awaits all beauty. Loving tenderness, when you fall asleep in the other's arms, is like Noah's cloak cast over these unpleasant considerations. But Lacan also thinks quite the opposite, that love reaches out towards the ontological. While desire focuses on the other, always in a somewhat fetishist manner, on particular objects, like breasts, buttocks and cock... love focuses on the very being of the other, on the other as it has erupted, fully armed with its being, into my life thus disrupted and re-fashioned.

*What you are really saying is that there are very contradictory philosophical interpretations when it comes to love?*

Principally three. First, there is the romantic interpretation that focuses on the ecstasy of the encounter. Secondly, what we referred briefly to when discussing the Meetic dating agency, the interpretation based on a commercial or legal-istic perspective, which argues that love must in the end be a contract. A contract between two free individuals who would presumably declare that they love each other, though they never forget the necessary equality of the relationship, the system of mutual benefits, etc. Finally, there is the sceptical interpretation that turns love into an illusion. My own philosophical view is attempting to say that love cannot be reduced to any of these approximations and is a quest for truth. What kind of truth? you will ask. I mean truth in relation to something quite precise: what kind of world does one see when one experiences it from the point of view of two and not one? What is the world like when it is experienced, developed and lived from the point of view of difference and not identity? That is what I believe love to be. It is the project, naturally including sexual desire in all its facets, including the birth of a child, but also a thousand other things, in fact, anything from the moment our lives are challenged by the perspective of difference.

*Given that love, according to you, is a manner of experiencing the world on the basis of difference, why don't you share the view of the philosopher Emmanuel Levinas, namely that the person in love experiences in the person he or she loves not "a quality that is different from any other, but the very quality of difference"? Why don't you accept that love is an experience of the other?*

I think that it is essential to grasp that the construction of the world on the basis of difference is quite distinct from the experience of difference. Levinas's vision starts from the irreducible experience of the face of the other, an epiphany that is grounded in God as "the Almighty Other". The experience of otherness is central, because it is the foundation stone of ethics. In a great religious tradition, love also becomes an ethical sentiment *par excellence*. In my view, there is nothing particularly "ethical" about love as such. I really don't like all these theological ruminations inspired by love, even though I know they have made a great impact on history. I can only see the ultimate revenge of One over Two. I believe there really is an encounter with the other, but an encounter is not an experience, it is an event that remains quite opaque and only finds reality in its multiple resonances within the real world. Nor can I see love as an experience of "communion", namely, an experience in which I forget myself on behalf of the other, that is a model in this world of what will finally lead me to the Almighty Other. At the end of *Faust*, Goethe was already asserting that "the eternal feminine takes us Above". I'm sorry, but I find such statements rather obscene. Love doesn't take me "above" or indeed "below". It is an existential project: to construct a world from a decentred point of view other than that of my mere impulse to survive or re-affirm my own identity.

Here, I am opposing "construction" to "experience". When I lean on the shoulder of the woman I love, and can see, let's say, the peace of twilight over a mountain landscape, gold-green fields, the shadow of trees, black-nosed sheep motionless behind hedges and the sun about to disappear behind craggy peaks, and know – not from the expression on her face, but from within the world as it is – that the woman I love is seeing the same world, and that this convergence is part of the world and that love constitutes precisely, at that very moment, the paradox of an identical difference, then love exists, and promises to continue to exist. The fact is she and I are now incorporated into this unique Subject, the Subject of love that views the panorama of the world through the prism of our difference, so this world can be conceived, be born, and not simply represent what fills my own individual gaze. Love is always the possibility of being present at the birth of the world. The birth of a child, if born from within love, is yet another example of this possibility.

# III

# THE CONSTRUCTION OF LOVE

❧

*Let's now turn to your own conception of love. We have mentioned that Rimbaud wanted to re-invent love. But re-invent it starting out from which idea about love?*

I think we should approach the question of love from two points that correspond to everyone's experience. Firstly, love involves a separation or disjuncture based on the simple difference between two people and their infinite subjectivities. This disjuncture is, in most cases, sexual difference. When that isn't the case, love still ensures that two figures, two different interpretive stances are set in opposition. In other words, love contains an initial element that separates, dislocates and differentiates. You have *Two*. Love involves Two.

The second point is that precisely because it encompasses a disjuncture, at the moment when this Two appear on stage as such and experience the world in a new way, it can only assume a risky or contingent form. That is what we know as "the encounter". Love always starts with an encounter. And I would give this encounter the quasi-metaphysical status of an *event*, namely of something that doesn't enter into the immediate order of things. There are innumerable examples in art or literature that describe such a starting-point for love. Many stories or novels focus on cases where Two are particularly marked out, when the two lovers don't belong to the same class, group, clan or country. *Romeo and Juliet* is clearly the outstanding allegory for this particular disjuncture because this Two belong to enemy camps. We shouldn't underestimate the power love possesses to slice diagonally through the most powerful oppositions and radical separations. The encounter between two differences is an event, is contingent and disconcerting, "love's surprises", theatre yet again. On the basis of this event, love can start and flourish. It is the first, absolutely essential point. This surprise unleashes a process that is basically an experience of getting to know the world. Love isn't simply about two people meeting and their inward-looking relationship: it is a construction, a life that is being made, no longer from the perspective of One but from the perspective of Two. And that is what I have called a "Two scene". Personally, I have always been interested in issues of duration and process, and not only starting-points.

ALAIN BADIOU

❧

*According to you, love can't be restricted to the meeting, but takes shape over time. Why do you reject the fusion interpretation of love?*

I think many people still cling to a romantic conception of love that in a way absorbs love in the encounter. Love is simultaneously ignited, consummated and consumed in the meeting, in a magical moment outside the world as it really is. Something happens that is in the nature of a miracle, an existential intensity, an encounter leading to meltdown. But when things happen that way, we aren't witnessing a "Two scene" but a "One scene". It is the meltdown concept of love: the two lovers met and something like a heroic act for One was enacted against the world. In Romantic mythology we can see how this point of fusion very often leads to death. There is a close and profound link between love and death, the highest point of which no doubt is Richard

Wagner's *Tristan and Isolde*, because love is consumed in the ineffable, exceptional moment of the encounter, after which it is impossible to go back to a world that remains external to the relationship.

This is a radically Romantic interpretation that I think we need to challenge. It is artistically extremely beautiful but, in my opinion, it is existentially seriously lacking. I believe we should accept it as a powerful artistic myth, but not as a genuine philosophy of love. After all, love takes place in the world. It is an event that can't be predicted or calculated in terms of the world's laws. Nothing enables one to pre-arrange the encounter – not even Meetic, and all those long, preparatory chats!: in the end, the moment you see each other in the flesh, you see each other, and that's that, and it's out of control! However, love cannot be reduced to the first encounter, because it is a construction. The enigma in thinking about love is the duration of time necessary for it to flourish. In fact, it isn't the ecstasy of those beginnings that is remarkable. The latter are clearly ecstatic, but love is above all a construction that lasts. We could say that love is a tenacious adventure. The adventurous side is necessary, but equally so is the need for tenacity. To give up at the first hurdle, the first serious disagreement, the first quarrel, is only to distort love. Real love is one that triumphs lastingly, sometimes painfully, over the hurdles erected by time, space and the world.

*And what is this construction like?*

The storybooks are pretty silent on that front, aren't they? The end of the story says, "They got married and had lots of children". Yes, sure, but is love simply about getting married? And having lots of children? Such an explanation is rather

# IN PRAISE OF LOVE

superficial and hackneyed. The idea that love is exclusively fulfilled or enacted via the creation of a family universe is far from satisfactory. Not that the family universe isn't part of love – I, for one, certainly think it is – but it can't be reduced to that. We should understand that the birth of a child is part of love, but shouldn't then conclude that the birth of a child is the fulfilment of love. I am really interested in the time love endures. Let's be more precise: by "endure" one should not simply understand that love lasts, that love is forever or always. One has to understand that love invents a different way of lasting in life. That everyone's existence, when tested by love, confronts a new way of experiencing time. Of course, if we echo the poet, love is also the "the dour desire to endure". But, more than that, it is the desire for an unknown duration. Because, as we all know, love is a re-invention of life. To re-invent love is to re-invent that re-invention.

# ALAIN BADIOU

*In your book,* Conditions, *you challenge a number of enduring ideas about love, notably the idea that the feeling of being in love is an illusion, a concept central to the pessimistic tradition of the French moralists, according to which love is but "the decorative façade via which the reality of sex asserts itself" or which considers that "love is essentially desire and sexual jealousy". Why do you criticise this conception?*

This moralist concept belongs to a tradition of scepticism. This philosophy claims that love doesn't really exist and is merely camouflaging desire. Desire is the only thing that really exists. According to this vision, love is merely something the imagination constructs to give a veneer to sexual desire. This idea, that has a long history, encourages everybody to be suspicious about love. It also belongs to the language of safety-first, because it is basically saying: "Listen, if

## IN PRAISE OF LOVE

you have sexual desires, fulfil them. But there's no need to get hooked on the idea that you have to love someone. Forget all that and just do it!" However, in that case, I would say that love is being undermined – or de-constructed, if you like – in the name of the reality of sex.

In this respect, I would like to refer to my own experience. I know, I think, like almost everyone else, about the drive and insistence of sexual desire. Age doesn't let me forget that. I also know that love inscribes the fulfilment of this desire within the course of its own development. And this is important, because, as the literature says from time immemorial, the fulfilment of sexual desire also functions like one of those rare material proofs, totally linked to the body, that love is more than a mere declaration of words. A declaration of the "I love you" kind seals the act of the encounter, is central and constitutes a commitment. But surrendering your body, taking your clothes off, being naked for the other, rehearsing those hallowed gestures, renouncing all embarrassment, shouting, all this involvement of the body is evidence of a surrender to love. It crucially distinguishes it from friendship. Friendship doesn't involve bodily contact, or any resonances in pleasure of the body. That's why it is a more intellectual attachment, and one that philosophers who are suspicious of passion have always preferred. Love, particularly over time, embraces all the positive aspects of friendship but love relates to the totality of the being of the other, and the surrender of the body becomes the material symbol of that totality. People can say: "That's not true! It is desire and desire alone that's at work there." I would maintain that, within the framework of a love that declares itself, this declaration, even if it remains latent, is what produces the effects of desire, and not desire itself. Love proves itself by permeating desire. The ritual of bodies is then the material expression of the word, it communicates the idea that the promise to re-invent life will be fulfilled, initially in terms of the body. But even in their wildest delirium, lovers know that love is there, like their bodies' guardian angel, when they wake up in the morning, when peace descends over the proof that their bodies have grasped that love has been declared.

That is why I believe love cannot be and isn't for anyone, apart from the ideologues keen to erase it, a mere cloak for sexual desire, a sophisticated, chimerical ploy to ensure the survival of the species.

# IV

# THE TRUTH OF LOVE

*You were reminding us earlier that Plato had
already identified the particular link that exists
between love and truth. But in what way do you
think that love is a "truth procedure"?*

I believe that love is indeed what I call in my own
philosophical jargon a "truth procedure", that is,
an experience whereby a certain kind of truth is
constructed. This truth is quite simply the truth
about Two: the truth that derives from difference
as such. And I think that love – what I call the
"Two scene" – is this experience. In this sense,
all love that accepts the challenge, commits to

enduring, and embraces this experience of the world from the perspective of difference produces in its way a new truth about difference.

That is why love that is real is always of interest to the whole of humanity, however humble, however hidden, that love might seem on the surface. We know how people get carried away by love stories! A philosopher must ask why that happens. Why are there so many films, novels, and songs that are entirely given over to love stories? There must be something universal about love for these stories to interest such an enormous audience. What is universal is that all love suggests a new experience of truth about what it is to be two and not one. That we can encounter and experience the world other than through a solitary consciousness: any love whatsoever gives us new evidence of this. And that is why we like to love; as St Augustine says, we like to love, but we also like others to love us: quite simply because we love truths. That is what gives philosophy its meaning: people like truths, even when they don't know that they like them.

*It seems that this truth needs to be spoken, and you have talked about love that is "declared". According to you, of necessity, there is a stage in love when love is declared. Why is it so vital for love to be spoken?*

Because the declaration is inscribed in the structure of the event itself. First, you have an encounter. I pointed out how love begins with the wholly contingent, random character of the encounter. These really are games of love and chance. And they are unavoidable. They always exist, despite that publicity hype I mentioned. But chance, at a given moment, must be curbed. It must turn into a process that can last. This is a very difficult, almost metaphysical problem:

how can what is pure chance at the outset
become the fulcrum for a construction of truth?
How can something that was basically unpredictable and seemed tied to the unpredictable
vagaries of existence nevertheless become the
entire meaning of two lives that have met, paired
off, that will engage in the extended experience of the constant (re)-birth of the world via
the mediation of the difference in their gazes?
How do you move from a mere encounter to the
paradox of a single world where it is revealed
that we are two? It is a complete mystery. And
this is what really nourishes scepticism about
love. People will say, why talk about great truth
in respect of the quite banal fact that So and So
met his or her colleague at work? That's exactly
what we must emphasise: an apparently insig-
nificant act, but one that is a really radical event
in life at a micro-level, bears universal meaning
in the way it persists and endures.

Nevertheless, it is right that "chance must be curbed". It is something Mallarmé said: "Chance is at last curbed..." He says it about poetry, not about love. But his words can be quite usefully applied to love and the declaration of love, with the terrible difficulties and varieties of anguish they bring. Besides, the affinities between poems and declarations of love are well known. In both cases, huge risks are involved that are dependent on language itself. It is about uttering a word the effects of which, in existence, can be almost infinite. That is also the desire driving a poem. The simplest words become charged with an intensity that is almost intolerable. To make a declaration of love is to move on from the event-encounter to embark on a construction of truth. The chance nature of the encounter morphs into the assumption of a beginning. And often what starts there lasts so long, is so charged with novelty and experience of the world that

## IN PRAISE OF LOVE

in retrospect it doesn't seem at all random and contingent, as it appeared initially, but almost a necessity. That is how chance is curbed: the absolute contingency of the encounter with someone I didn't know finally takes on the appearance of destiny. The declaration of love marks the transition from chance to destiny, and that's why it is so perilous and so burdened with a kind of horrifying stage fright. Moreover, the declaration of love isn't necessarily a one-off; it can be protracted, diffuse, confused, entangled, stated and re-stated, and even destined to be re-stated yet again. That is the moment when chance is curbed, when you say to yourself: I must tell the other person about what happened, about that encounter and the incidents within the encounter. I will tell the other that something that commits me took place, at least as I see it. In a word: I love you. If "I love you" isn't simply a ploy to sleep with somebody, which can be the case. If it isn't a ploy, what is it? What's being said there? It isn't at all easy to say "I love you". That small sentence is usually thought to be completely meaningless and banal. Moreover, people sometimes prefer to use other more poetic, less commonplace words to say "I love you". But what they are always saying is: I shall extract something else from what was mere chance. I'm going to extract something that will endure, something that will persist, a commitment, a fidelity. And here I am using the word "fidelity" within my own philosophical jargon, stripped of its usual connotations. It means precisely that transition from random encounter to a construction that is resilient, as if it had been necessary.

*In this context, I would like to quote from the very beautiful work by André Gorz,* Letter to D., *the declaration of love made by the philosopher to his wife, Dorine, and the narration of a love that, if I*

*may say so, has always endured: its opening lines*
*are, "You'll soon be eighty-two. You have shrunk*
*six centimetres, you only weigh forty-five kilos yet*
*you are as beautiful, gracious and desirable as ever.*
*We have now lived together for fifty-eight years and*
*I love you more than ever. In the hollow of my chest*
*I can feel again that ravaging emptiness that can*
*only be filled by the warmth of your body against*
*mine." What meaning do you give to fidelity?*

Isn't the meaning of fidelity much broader than
the simple promise not to sleep with someone else?
Doesn't it in fact show that the initial "I love you"
is a commitment requiring no particular conse-
cration, the commitment to construct something
that will endure in order to release the encounter
from its randomness? Mallarmé saw a poem as
"chance defeated word by word". In love, fidelity
signifies this extended victory: the randomness
of an encounter defeated day after day through

the invention of what will endure, through the birth of a world. Why do people so often say: I will always love you? Provided, of course, that it isn't a ploy. The moralists have naturally mocked that, saying it is never in fact true. Firstly, it isn't true that it is never true. There are people who always love each other, and a lot more than you might think or say.

Everybody knows that deciding to break off such love, particularly unilaterally, is always a disaster, whatever the excellent reasons put forward to support such a move. I have only once in my life given up on a love. It was my first love, and then gradually I became so aware this step had been a mistake that I tried to recover that initial love, late, very late – the death of the loved one was approaching – but with a unique intensity and feeling of necessity. Subsequently, I have never renounced a love. There have been dramas and heart wrenching and doubts, but I

4 7

have never again abandoned a love. And I feel really assured by the fact that the women I have loved I have loved for always. So I have personal reasons for knowing that the sceptics' barb is far from the truth. And secondly, if "I love you" is always, in most respects, the heralding of "I'll always love you", it is in effect locking chance into the framework of eternity. We shouldn't be afraid of words. The locking in of chance is an anticipation of eternity. And to an extent, every love states that it is eternal: it is assumed within the declaration...

The problem then resides in inscribing this eternity within time. Because, basically, that is what love is: a declaration of eternity to be fulfilled or unfurled as best it can be within time: eternity descending into time. That's why it is such an intense feeling. In the end, you know, the sceptics even make us laugh, because, if one tried to give up love, to stop believing in it, it would be a genuine, subjective disaster and everybody knows this. Life, one must say, would become very grey. So love remains powerful, subjectively powerful: one of those rare experiences where, on the basis of chance inscribed in a moment, you attempt a declaration of eternity. "Always" is the word used to declare eternity. Because you cannot know what that "always" means or how long it will last. "Always" means "eternally". It is simply a commitment within time, because you have to be a Claudel to believe that love endures beyond time, in the fabulous world of the after-life. But love, the essence of which is fidelity in the meaning I give to this word, demonstrates how eternity can exist within the time span of life itself. Happiness, in a word! Yes, happiness in love is the proof that time can accommo-date eternity. And you can also find proof in the political enthusiasm you feel when participating in a revolutionary act, in the pleasure given by works of art and the almost supernatural joy you experience when you at last grasp in depth the meaning of a scientific theory.

*Let's assume that love is the advent of Two as such, the "Two scene". What about the child? Won't a child alter or change this "Two scene"? Isn't he the "One" who will bring together the "Two" of the lovers, but also a "Three" who can extend yet also separate them?*

This is both a profound and interesting question. An erudite friend of mine, a practising Jew, Jérome Bennaroch partly accepts my thesis about love. He always tells me: yes, love is proof of Two, it is their declaration and eternity but there comes a moment when Two must pass their test in the order of One. That is, it must return to One. The at once symbolic and real figure for this One is the child. And love's true goal remains the existence of the child as *the* expression of the One. I have challenged his objection empirically on a number of fronts, in particular because it would require the denial of the amorous nature of sterile couples, of homosexuals, etc. Then, at a deeper level, I told him: the child is indeed part of the space marked out by love, and as such constitutes "a point" in terms of my own jargon. A point, namely a particular moment around which an event establishes itself, where it must be re-played in some way, as if it were returning in a changed, displaced form, but one forcing you "to declare afresh". A point, in effect, comes when the consequences of a construction of a truth, whether it be political, amorous, artistic or scientific, suddenly compels you to opt for a radical choice, as if you were back at the beginning, when you accepted and declared the event. Once more you must say, "I accept this chance, want it and take it on board". In the case of love, you must, often very urgently, re-make your declaration. You could even say: you must (re-)make the point. And I think that's what a child, the desire to have a child, and the birth is. It forms part of the process of love, clearly, in the shape of a point of support for love. We know that a birth, at once a miracle and a challenge, is a test for all couples. It becomes necessary to redeploy Two around the child, precisely because he is One. Two cannot continue to experience each other in the world as they did before they were challenged on this point.

I don't at all deny that love is sequential, in other words, that it's not autonomous. There are points, tests, temptations and new appearances, and, each time, you must replay the "Two scene", find the terms for a new declaration. After the initial declaration, love too must also be "re-stated". And that is why love is also the source of violent existential crises. Like all

ALAIN BADIOU

processes involving the search for truth. From this perspective, moreover, there is also a striking similarity between politics and love.

# V

# LOVE AND POLITICS

*What is the relationship between politics and love?
Is it that politics also involves events, declarations
and fidelities?*

In my view politics constitutes a truth procedure, but one that centres on the collective. I mean that political action tests out the truth of what the collective is capable of achieving. For example, can it embrace equality? Can it integrate what is heterogeneous? Can it accept that there is only one world? Things of this kind. The essence of politics can be subsumed in the question: what are individuals capable of when they meet, organize, think and take decisions? In love, it is about two people being able to handle difference and make it creative. In politics, it is about finding out whether a number of people, a mass of people in fact, can create equality. And just as the family exists at the level of love to socialize its impact, at the level of politics the power of the State exists to repress its enthusiasms. The same prickly relation exists between politics as a practical, collective way of thinking through the issue of power with the State as the instrument for its management and regulation, and the issue of love with the unbridled invention of Two and the family as the fundamental unit of ownership and egotism.

Essentially, if you play with the word "state" you could define the family as the State of love. For example, when you participate in a political mass movement you experience the very significant tension between the question, "what is

❧

the collective capable of?" and the power and authority of the State. The upshot is that the State is almost always about the betrayal of political hope. Should I now assert that the family is always about the betrayal of love? It is clear that the question has to be asked. The way I see it, it only impacts point by point, and decision by decision. There is the point of sexual invention, of children, of work, of friends, of nights out, of holidays, of whatever. And restricting all these points to the remit of the declaration of love is no straightforward matter. Similarly in politics, there are the points of state power, frontiers, laws and the police and it is never easy to keep them within an open, egalitarian, revolutionary political framework.

In both cases, we have point-by-point processes and they formed the basis of my argument against my religious friend. Don't mistake the experience for the final aim. Politics can probably never be realised without the state, but that doesn't mean that power is its goal. Its goal is to discover what the collective is capable of, not power itself. Similarly, in love, the aim is to experience the world from the point of view of difference, point by point, and not simply to ensure the reproduction of the species. A sceptical moralist will find justification for his pessimism in the family, as proof that, in the end, love is simply a ploy to ensure the reproduction of the species and society's ploy to ensure privileges are inherited. But I won't accept his proposition. Nor will I accept my friend Bennaroch's view that love's splendid creation of the power of Two is duty bound to genuflect before the majesty of One.

*Why then can't you envisage a "politics of love", just as Jacques Derrida outlined a "politics of friendship"?**

I don't think that you can mix up love and politics. In my opinion, the "politics of love" is a meaningless expression. I think that when you begin to say "Love one another", that can lead to a kind of ethics, but not to any kind of politics. Principally because there are people in politics one doesn't love... That's undeniable. Nobody can expect us to love them.

*So unlike love, politics is all about a confrontation between enemies?*

Well, you know, look, in love, at the absolute difference that exists between two individuals, one of the biggest differences one can imagine, given that it is an infinite difference, yet an encounter,

*The Politics of Friendship*, Jacques Derrida, trans. George Collins (Verso, 2005). See also *Friendship*, Giorgio Agamben, trans. David Kishik and Stefan Pedatella, in "What is an Apparatus?" and other essays (Stanford University Press, 2009) and by the same author, *L'Ombre de l'amour. Le concept d'amour chez Heidegger*, Payot & Rivages, 2003.

a declaration and fidelity can transform that into a creative existence. Nothing of the sort can happen in politics in terms of the basic contradictions, the upshot being that in effect there are clearly designated enemies. A central issue in political thought is the question of enemies and it is very difficult to deal with today, in part because of the democratic framework within which we operate. The issue is: do enemies exist? I mean by that, real enemies. A real enemy is not someone you are resigned to see take power periodically because lots of people voted for him. That is a person you are annoyed to see as head of State because you would have preferred his adversary. And you will wait your turn, for five or ten years or more. An enemy is something else: an individual you won't tolerate taking decisions on anything that impacts on yourself. So do real enemies exist or not? That should be our starting-point.

## IN PRAISE OF LOVE

❧❧

It is an extremely important issue in politics and one we are too quick to push to one side. The issue of the enemy is completely foreign to the question of love. In love, you can find hurdles, be haunted by immanent dramas, but there are in fact, no enemies. One might object: what about my rival? The person my lover prefers to me? Well, that is an entirely totally different matter. In politics, the struggle against the enemy constitutes the action. The enemy forms part of the essence of politics. Genuine politics identifies its real enemy. However, the rival remains absolutely external, he isn't part of the definition of love. On this point I disagree profoundly with all those who think that jealousy is a constituent element of love. The most brilliant representative of the latter is Proust, for whom jealousy is the real, intense, demonic content of amorous subjectivity. In my opinion, this is simply a variant of the thesis of the sceptical moralists. Jealousy is a fake parasite that feeds on love and doesn't at all help to define it. Must every love identify an external rival before it can declare itself, before it can begin? No way! The reverse is the case: the immanent difficulties of love, the internal contradictions of the Two scene can crystallize around a third party, a rival, imagined or real. The difficulties love harbours don't stem from the existence of an enemy who has been identified. They are internal to the process: the creative play of difference. Selfishness, not any rival, is love's enemy. One could say: my love's main enemy, the one I must defeat, is not the other, it is myself, the "myself" that prefers identity to difference, that prefers to impose its world against the world re-constructed through the filter of difference.

*Love can also be war...*

# IN PRAISE OF LOVE

❧

We must bear in mind that, like many processes for finding the truth, the process of love isn't always peaceful. It can bring violent argument, genuine anguish and separations we may or may not overcome. We should recognize that it is one of the most painful experiences in the subjective life of an individual! That is why some people promote their "comprehensive insurance" propaganda. I have already mentioned that people die because of love. There are murders and suicides prompted by love. In fact, at its own level, love is not necessarily any more peaceful than revolutionary politics. A truth is not something that is constructed in a garden of roses. Never! Love has its own agenda of contradictions and violence. But the difference is that in politics we really have to engage with our enemies, whereas in love it is all about dramas, immanent, internal dramas that don't really define any enemies, though they do sometimes place the drive for identity into conflict with difference. Dramas in love are the sharpest experience of the conflict between identity and difference.

*Even so, isn't it at all possible to bring love and politics together without descending into the moralizing of a politics of love?*

There are two political, or philosophical-political notions one can compare at a purely formal level to the dialectics present within love. Firstly, the word "communism" encompasses this idea that the collectivity is capable of integrating all extrapolitical differences. People shouldn't be prevented from participating in a political process of a communist type simply because they are this or that, or were born here or come from elsewhere, or speak such and such a language, or were fashioned by such and such a culture, in the same way that identities in themselves aren't

# IN PRAISE OF LOVE

꧁꧂

hurdles to the creation of love. Only political difference with the enemy is "irreconcilable" as Marx said. And that has no equivalent in the process of love. And then there is the word "fraternity". "Fraternity" is the most opaque of the three terms in the Republican motto. We can argue about "freedom", but we know what that's about. We can provide a fairly accurate definition of what "equality" involves. But what on earth is "fraternity"? No doubt it is related to the issue of differences, of their friendly co-presence within the political process, the essential boundary being the confrontation with the enemy. And that is a notion that can be covered by internationalism, because, if the collective can really take equality on board, that means it can also integrate the most extensive divergences and greatly limit the power of identity.

## ALAIN BADIOU

❧

*At the beginning of our dialogue, you spoke of Christianity as a "religion of love". Let's now focus on the avatars of love within the great ideologies. In your view, how did Christianity manage to capture the extraordinary power that love has?*

In this respect, I think that Judaism quite prepared the way for Christianity. The presence of love in the Old Testament is significant, both in terms of prescriptions and descriptions. Whatever its theological import, the song of love that is The Song of Songs is one of the most powerful celebrations of love ever written. Christianity itself is the finest example of the use of love's intensity towards a transcendental conception of the universal. Christianity says: if you love each other, the whole of this loving community will approach the ultimate fount of all love that is divine transcendence itself. It introduces the idea that the acceptance of the experience of love, of the experience of the other, of the gaze raised towards the other, contributes to this supreme love that is both the love we owe to God and the love that God brings to us. And, of course, that is a stroke of genius! Christianity has managed to capture on behalf of its Church – its avatar of the state – this power that has enabled it, for example, to achieve the acceptance of suffering in the name of the supreme interests of the community and not just on behalf of individual survival.

Christianity grasped perfectly that there is an element in the apparent contingency of love that can't be reduced to that contingency. But it immediately raised it to the level of tran-scendence, and that is the root of the problem. This universal element I too recognize in love as immanent. But Christianity has somehow managed to elevate it and refocus it onto a tran-scendent power. It's an ideal that was already partly present in Plato, through the idea of the Good. It is a brilliant first manipulation of the power of love and one we must now bring back to earth. I mean we must demonstrate that love really does have universal power, but that it is simply the opportunity we are given to enjoy a positive, creative, affirmative experience of difference. The Other, no doubt, but without the "Almighty-Other", without the "Great Other" of transcendence. In the final analysis, religions don't speak of love. Because they are only interested in it as a source of intensity, in the subjective state it alone can create, in order to direct that intensity towards faith and the Church and encourage this subjective state to accept the sovereignty of God. The main outcome is that Christianity substitutes devout, passive, deferential love for the combative love I am praising here, that earthly creation of the differentiated birth of a new world and a happiness won point

## IN PRAISE OF LOVE

❦

by point. Love on bended knee is no love at all as far as I am concerned, even if love sometimes arouses passion in us that makes us yield to the loved one.

*You have worked with Antoine Vitez, notably when he was preparing his famous production of Paul Claudel's* The Satin Slipper. *Does the meditation on love by the author of* The Break of Noon, *that is so imbued with Christianity, have anything to say to people nowadays who are mostly no longer Christian?*

Claudel is a great dramatist of love. *The Satin Slipper* and *The Break of Noon* are wholly devoted to this theme. However, what is there in Claudel that can interest us now that we are no longer directly stirred by the communion of the saints, rewards for good deeds and salvation in the after-life? I can only think of that sentence at the end of *The Break of Noon*: "Far apart, though never ceasing to burden each other, will we have to bear our strife-ridden souls?" Claudel is particularly sensitive to the fact that true love is always overcoming the impossible: "Far apart, though never ceasing to burden each other..." Strictly speaking, love isn't a possibility, but rather the overcoming of something that might appear to be impossible. Something exists that had no reason to, which was never offered to you as a possibility. That's also another reason why the internet dating hype is fallacious. It works on the assumption that you are going to review all the possibilities on offer and take the best, in order to enjoy safe love. But life's not like that! It's not like the stories where the pretenders come queueing. Love begins when something impossible is overcome, and with the theme of the forbidden woman Claudel is a great poet of the impossible, At the same time in Claudel, the dice are always slightly loaded, since what's impossible is relative because it is terrestrial. I think he has two "Two scenes" rather than one. The first is the experience of love's impossibility on earth. The second is when Two are reconciled in the universe of the faith.

It is fascinating to follow through the magnificent poetic mechanisms he uses to enable the power of the first scene to enrich the second. That is what Christianity is about. It promotes itself through the earthly power of love by saying: "Yes, certain things are impossible even though it's so powerful, but not to worry because what's impossible down here isn't necessarily so in the after-life." Very basic but very potent propaganda.

*This wish to bring love down to earth, to move from transcendence to immanence, was central to historical communism. In what way might the reactivating of the Communist hypothesis be a way to re-invent love?*

I referred earlier to what I think of these political uses of the word "love", and how they are as misguided as religious uses. Nevertheless, here too we are dealing, quite remarkably, with a transcendent force that is grasping the power of love. It is not God any longer, but the Party, and through the Party, its supreme leader. The expression "the cult of the personality" sums up this kind of collective transfer of love to a political figure. Poets have joined in: look at Éluard's canticles to Stalin, Aragon's hymns to the return of Maurice Thorez to France after his illness... I find the cult of the Party as such even more interesting. There again, Aragon is symptomatic: "My Party brought the colours of France back to me", etc. We immediately see love being modulated. Whether written for the

IN PRAISE OF LOVE

Party or his lover, Elsa Triolet, the words are very similar. It is instructive to see how the party that one might have thought was simply a transitory instrument for the emancipation of the working and popular classes thus becomes a fetish. I don't want to make fun of any of that: it was an era of political passion that we can't continue, that we must now view critically, but it was intense and counted its faithful in their millions. What we must say, as love is our theme, is that love and political passion should never be confused. The problem politics confronts is the control of hatred, not of love. And hatred is a passion that almost inevitably poses the question of the enemy. In other words, in politics, where enemies do exist, one role of the organization, whatever that may be, is to control, indeed to destroy, the consequences of hatred. That doesn't mean it must "preach love", but a major intellectual challenge it faces is to provide the most limited, precise definition possible of the political enemy. And not, as was the case throughout almost the whole of the last century, the vaguest, most far-reaching definition imaginable.

*Would it be better to separate love from politics?*

A large swathe of contemporary thought strives to separate what has been wrongfully brought together. In the same way that the definition of the enemy must be controlled, limited, reduced to a minimum, love, as a singular adventure in the quest for truth about difference, must also be rigorously separated from politics. When I talk of the Communist hypothesis, I simply want to suggest that future forms of the politics of emancipation must be inscribed in a resurrection, a re-affirmation, of the Communist idea, the idea of a world that isn't given over to the avarice of private property, a world of free association and equality. To that end, we can draw on new philo-sophical tools and a good number of localised political experiences, where there has been inno-vative thinking. In such a framework, it will be easier to re-invent love than if surrounded by capitalist frenzy. Because we can be sure that nothing disinterested can be at ease amid such frenzy. And love, like any process in the search for truth, is essentially disinterested: its value resides in itself alone and goes beyond the immediate interests of the two individuals involved. The meaning of the word "communism" doesn't immediately relate to love. Nonetheless, the word brings with it new possibilities for love.

*There is another possible dimension to the avatars of love within a Communist politics. These are love stories that are built against a background of strikes and other social movements. You often emphasize this dimension, since it allows the transgression of*

*love to ally itself with the political transgression of
the moment. What is the specificity of these loves
in struggle?*

I am particularly sensitive to this aspect of things
because I have devoted a considerable part of
my writing as a novelist and dramatist to the
subject. In my play *L'Écharpe Rouge*, the story
mainly concerns the distant loves of a brother
and sister in all the incarnations of a huge
political movement that involves wars of liberation, strikes, mass-meetings... In my novel *Calme
bloc ici-bas* – which follows the formal structure
of Hugo's *Les Misérables* – the revolutionary
fresco encompasses the love of a Shi'ite worker,
Ahmed Aazami, for a terrorist, Élisabeth Cathely,
then, that of Élisabeth's son, Simon, adopted by
Ahmed after the terrorist's death, for Claude
Ogasawara, the poet and daughter of a leading
reactionary. In all these instances, my intention

isn't to highlight the similarity between love and revolutionary commitment, but the kind of secret resonance that is created, in the most intimate individual experience, between the intensity life acquires when a hundred per cent committed to a particular Idea and the qualitatively distinct intensity generated by the struggle with differ-ence in love. It is like two musical instruments that are completely different in tone and volume, but which mysteriously converge when unified by a great musician in the same work. I would like to make a qualified revelation here. I have inscribed in these works a balance sheet of my life in the "red years" between May '68 and the Eighties. That is the period when I developed the political conviction I have remained impla-cably loyal to and for which "communism" is one possible name. But I then equally structured my future life around processes of love that were by and large definitive. What came later, of the same order, was illuminated by that inspiration and its enduring nature. In particular, as I have already mentioned, conviction in love and politics, something one must never renounce. That was really the moment when, in between politics and love, my life found the musical chord that ensured its harmony.

# VI

# LOVE AND ART

*In* The Century, *you discuss an André Breton text,* Arcanum 17, *and show how the twentieth century was a great era for the promotion of love as a metaphor for truth. But what does André Breton mean when in* Soluble Fish, *he wishes to reduce "art to its simplest expression, namely, love"?** 

The central Surrealist project was the one we mentioned at the very beginning, namely, following Rimbaud's injunction, to re-invent love. And for the Surrealists this re-invention was

*\*Si vous aimez l'amour... Anthologie amoureuse du surréalisme edited by Vincent Gille, with a preface by Annie Le Brun, Syllepse, 2001.*

indissolubly an artistic, existential and political move. They didn't make any divisions between the three. Art has a very powerful point, in the sense that it does justice to events. That could even be a possible definition of art: art is what, at the level of thought, does complete justice to the event. In politics, events are ordered by history in retrospect. But art is alone in restoring or attempting to restore completely their intense power. Only art restores the dimension of the senses to an encounter, an insurrection or a riot. Art, in all its forms, is a great reflection on the event as such. A great painting is the capture by its own means of something that cannot be reduced to what it displays. The latent event emerges and, we might say, breaks through what you can see. Breton reminds us, from this point of view, that art is very closely linked to love, since the latter is basically the moment when an event breaks through existence. This explains "l'amour fou".

IN PRAISE OF LOVE

❦

Love cannot be reduced to any law. There is no law of love.

What's more, art has often demonstrated the asocial side of love. As the popular saying goes, after all, "lovers are on their own in this world". They alone possess that difference by which they experience the world. Surrealism exalts "l'amour fou" as the power of an event that is beyond any law. The thinking inspired by love is also thinking that is created against all order, against the powerful order of the law. The Surrealists found here a source of nourishment for their desire for a poetic revolution in language but also, I should emphasise, in existence. From this point of view, they were very interested in love and in sexuality, as a principle, as potential support for a revolution in existence. Conversely, they had little interest in that which endured. Above all, they championed love as a magnificent poem of the encounter. For example, in *Nadja*, which is a splendid illustration of the poetics of the uncertain and mysterious encounter that round the street-corner will become "l'amour fou". The pure encounter is the complete opposite of anything that is premeditated, but not at the level of what endures, or in any eternal dimension. However, some philosophers have maintained that eternity is the moment. We already find this idea in Greek thought. The only temporal dimension possible for eternity was the moment. That would support Breton. Naturally, the moment of the miraculous encounter promises the eternity of love, though what I want to suggest is a concept of love that is less miraculous and more hard work, namely a construction of eternity within time, of the experience of the Two, point by point. I go along with the miracle of the encounter, but I think it remains confined within Surrealist poetics if it is isolated, if we don't channel it towards the onerous development of a truth that is constructed point by point. "Onerous" must be taken here as something positive. There is a work of love: it is not simply a miracle. You must be in the breech, on guard: you must be at one with yourself and the other. You most think, act and change. And then, surely, happiness follows, as the immanent reward for all that work.

*I find it strange that you constantly refer to Samuel Beckett in respect of love. One can hardly say that Beckett's work is focused on happiness. In what way does his work, famed for its nihilism and pessimism, work, in your view, towards that "Two scene" that is love?*

As I've said, the literature on love contains very little in terms of the experience of its endurance over time. That's very striking. Take the theatre for example. If you watch plays that show the struggles of young lovers against the despotism of the family universe – a classic theme – you could give them all as sub-title Marivaux's *The Triumph of Love*. In this vein, many plays relate how these young people, often helped by valets or other accomplices, give the old parents the run around and finally get what they want, namely marriage. It's the triumph of love, but not its duration. That is precisely what you might call plotting the encounter. Important works, great novels, are often built around the impossibility of love, its being put to the test, its tragedy, its waning, its separation, end, etc. But there is very little on it lasting positively. We could even say married life has hardly produced a great work. It is a fact that it has rarely inspired artists.

However, it is precisely in the writing of Beckett, that renowned chronicler of despair, of the impossible, that we find something very apposite: he is also a writer of the obstinacy of love. Take for example the play *Happy Days*, the story of an old couple. You only see the woman, the man is crawling off-stage, everything is degenerating, she's in the process of sinking into the ground, but she says: "What happy days they were!" And she says that because love is still there. Love is the powerful, unchanging element that has structured her apparently catastrophic existence. Love is the hidden power within that catastrophe. In a splendid short text called *Enough*, Beckett relates the wanderings of a very old couple in a scenario that is at once mountainous and desert-like. It is a story of love, of the enduring of this old couple, that doesn't at all hide the disastrous state of their bodies, the monotony of their existence, the growing difficulty of sexuality, etc. The text narrates all that, but it sets the story within the ultimately magnificent power of love and the endurance it embodies.

❦

*As you have mentioned the art of drama, I would
like to mention a very special love you have nurtured
from childhood: a love for the theatre. Before you
wrote the trilogy about the Ahmeds, that brings
to the stage a kind of contemporary Scapin, you
yourself played the title role in Molière's* Les
Fourberies de Scapin *in your youth. What is the
nature of this enduring love of yours for the theatre?*

My love of the theatre is very complicated
and goes back a long time. It is probably more
powerful than my love of philosophy. My love for
philosophy comes later, more slowly and with
greater difficulty. When I was young and on
stage, I think I was fascinated by the immediate
feeling that some part of the language and
poetry is linked, almost inexplicably, to the body.
Essentially, perhaps the theatre was already
a metaphor for what love would become later
on, because it was that moment when thought

and body are in some way indistinguishable. They are exposed to the other in such a manner that you can't say, "This is a body" or "This is an idea". The two are mixed up, language seizes the body, just as when you tell someone, "I love you": you say that to someone living, standing there in front of you, but you are also addressing something that cannot be reduced to this simple material presence, something that is absolutely and simultaneously both beyond and within.

That is what the theatre is, in its origins, thinking-in-the body, embodied thought. As we know, there are rehearsals in the theatre. "Let's do it again", says the director. Thought doesn't come easily to the body. The relationship of a thought to space and movement is complicated. It must be at once spontaneous and pre-meditated. This is also what happens in love. Desire is immediately powerful but love also requires care and re-takes. Love knows all about the need

for re-working. 'Tell me again that you love me",
and very often, "Say it better". And desire begins
again. With caresses you'll hear, if they are driven
by love, "More! More!" that moment when the
eagerness for physical gestures is reinforced by
the insistence of a word, by a constantly renewed
*declaration*. We know that the theme of love as
a game is crucial in the theatre, and that it's all
precisely about declarations. It is also because
this theatre of love, this powerful game of love
and chance exists, that I have this love for the
theatre.

*The dramatist Antoine Vitez, the man who staged
your opera,* L'Écharpe Rouge, *in 1984, at the
Avignon Festival, to music by Georges Aperghis,
was also in favour of this idea. He wrote: "It's what
I've always wanted to do on stage: show the violent
thrust of ideas, how they bend and torment bodies".
Do you agree with him?*

# IN PRAISE OF LOVE

❧

Completely. You know, Pessoa, the Portuguese poet, says somewhere, "Love is a thought". That's a very paradoxical statement, because people have always said love is about the body, desire and feeling, everything but reason and thought. And he says, "Love is a thought". I think he's right. I think that love is a thought and that the relationship between that thought and the body is quite unique, and always marked, as Antoine Vitez said, by irrepressible violence. We experience that violence in life. It is absolutely true that love can bend our bodies and prompt the sharpest torment. Love, as we can observe day in day out, is not a long, quiet river. We can never forget the quite frightening number of loves that lead to suicide or murder. Love in the theatre is not only, or even mainly, sex farce or innocent romance: it is equally tragedy, rejection and rage. The relationship between the theatre and love is also the exploration of the abyss separating individuals, and the description of the fragile nature of the bridge that love throws between two solitudes. We must always return to this: what kind of thought reveals itself in the coming and going between two sexed bodies? We must also ask, and this makes relevant your previous question, what would the theatre have found to speak about if love hadn't existed. It would have spoken, and has spoken at great length, about politics. So we can say theatre is politics and love, and more generally, about the two intersecting. This intersection of politics and love is a possible definition of tragedy. But love of the theatre is necessarily also the love of love, because, without love stories, without the struggle to free love from the constraints of family, the theatre does not add up to much. Classical comedies, like Molière's plays, basically tell us how young people who have met by chance must undermine the marriage that's been arranged by their parents. The commonest, most exploited conflict on the stage is the struggle of chance love against implacable law. More subtly, it is the struggle of young people, helped by proletarians (slaves and servants), against the old, helped by Church and State. And now you will say, "Freedom has won out, arranged marriages no longer exist: the couple is pure creation." I'm not so sure. Freedom? What kind of freedom exactly? At what cost? Yes, that's a real question: what did love pay in the apparent gain of its freedom?

*Doesn't your love of the theatre also include the love of a community, a collective and an ensemble, since you once lived the life of the theatre company, among actors and technicians? Doesn't the theatre bear a love that belongs to the order of a fraternity?*

Yes, of course, that love exists! The theatre is a community and the aesthetic expression of fraternity. That's why I argue that there is, in that sense, something communist in all theatre. By "communist" I understand that which makes the held-in-common prevail over selfishness, the collective achievement over private self-interest. While we're about it, we can also say that love is communist in that sense, if one accepts, as I do, that the real subject of a love is the becoming of the couple and not the mere satisfaction of the individuals that are its component parts. Yet another possible definition of love: minimal communism!

To return to the theatre, I am always struck by the fact that the community of a theatre tour is also precarious. I'm thinking of the really distressing times when the community breaks up: you've been on tour, lived together for a month, and then, all of a sudden, you go your own way. The theatre involves this experience of separation. There are moments of great melancholia when the fraternity involved in performing and staging breaks up. "Here's my mobile number. We'll be in touch, right?": you are familiar with this ritual. But nobody will call, not really. It's the end and we go our separate ways. And the issue of separation is so important in love that one can also define love as a successful struggle against separation. The community of love is also precarious, and you also need much more than a telephone number to sustain and develop it.

*And what is the love of theatre like, from the inside, that is, from the point of view of the actor you once were and you'd perhaps like to be again, once more performing some of the monologues from* Ahmed le subtile *or* Ahmed philosophe?

It is a unique love that requires you to give up your own body in prey to language, in prey to ideas. As you know, every philosopher is an actor, however hostile he feels towards games and simulation. We have been speaking in public from the days of our great Greek ancestors. In philosophy there is always an element of baring oneself: the oral dimension of philosophy captured by the body, in an act of transfer. This was the point of a controversy I had with Jacques Derrida, who fought orality on behalf of the written, although he himself gave some wonderful performances. Philosophers have been much criticized for being magicians, for captivating people by artificial means and leading them to unlikely truths via the paths of seduction. Book V of Plato's *Republic* (this massive book of which I am preparing a complete, very different "translation") contains a quite astonishing passage. Socrates starts to define what is a true philosopher. And then very suddenly, he seems to change subject. Here is my version (Socrates is speaking):

# IN PRAISE OF LOVE

*"Do I need to remind you of something you must remember very vividly? When we speak of an object of love, we assume that the lover loves that object in its entirety. We don't allow for his love to select just one part and reject another."*

The two young people seem taken aback. Amantha takes it upon herself to express their bewilderment: "Dear Socrates, what is the connection between this detour on love and the definition of a philosopher?"

"Ah, our young women in love! Unable to recognize that, as Fernando Pessoa the great Portuguese poet said, 'love is a thought'. Listen, you youngsters: anyone who doesn't take love as their starting-point will never discover what philosophy is about."

It's true! We should follow our old master. One must start with love. We philosophers don't have that many means at our disposal; if we are deprived of the means of seduction, then we really will be disarmed. And being an actor is also about that! It is about seducing on behalf of something that, in the end, is a truth.

# IN CONCLUSION

*I want to return to this love that has to be re-invented and defended. In* The Meaning of Sarkozy *you argue that the re-invention of love is one possible point of resistance against the obscenity of the market and the current political disarray on the left. In your view, how might love constitute any kind of resistance to the world symbolized by the president of France?*

I think that it is vital to see that France is both the country of revolutions and a great land of reaction. This helps to understand France dialectically. I often argue about this with my foreign friends because they still entertain the myth of a wonderful France that is always on the brink of revolutionary inventions. So they were inevitably rather shocked by the election of Sarkozy, who doesn't at all fit into this perspective... I tell them that they construct a history of France in which the Enlightenment philosophers, Rousseau, the French Revolution, June '48, the Paris Commune, the Popular Front, the Resistance, the Liberation and May '68 follow each other. That's all well and good. But there is another side to the story: the Restoration of 1815, the Versaillais, the Holy Union during the Great War, Pétain, horrendous colonial wars... and Sarkozy. So there are two histories of France and they are entwined. Whenever great revolutionary hysteria runs riot, it is met with obsessive reaction. From this perspective, I think that love is also at stake.

Moreover, love has always been linked to

# IN PRAISE OF LOVE

❧

historical events. Romanticism in love is linked to the revolutions of the nineteenth century. André Breton is also the Popular Front, the Resistance, and the anti-Fascist struggle. May '68 was a great explosion of experiments in new takes on sexuality and love. But when the context becomes sombre and reactionary, attempts are made to bring identity back on the agenda. It can take different forms, but it is always identity. And Sarkozy wasn't slow off the mark. Target number one: workers from abroad. His instrument: savage, repressive legislation. He had already tried it on when he was Minister of the Interior. The discourse used conflates French and Western identities. He has no qualms about performing a little colonial number in relation to "African man". The reactionary project is always the defence of "our values", casting us in the mould of worldwide capitalism as the only possible identity. The impulse driving reaction is always a crude reference to identity in one form or another. Now, when the logic of identity wins the day, love is under threat. The way it is attracted to difference, its social dimension, and its wild, eventually violent side are under threat. They promote a "love" that is safe, in line with all their other security initiatives. So now it is urgent to defend love's subversive, heterogeneous relationship to the law. At the most minimal level, people in love put their trust in difference rather than being suspicious of it. Reactionaries are always suspicious of difference in the name of identity; that's their general philosophical starting-point. If we, on the contrary, want to open ourselves up to difference and its implications, so the collective can become the whole world, then the defence of love becomes one point individuals have to practise. The identity cult of repetition must be challenged by love of what is different, is unique, is unrepeatable, unstable and foreign. In 1982 in

❧

the *Theory of the Subject* I wrote: "Love what you will never see twice."

*Likewise it is in that sense that Jean-Luc Godard's film,* In Praise of Love, *the cinematic work in the form of a cantata that inspired the title for our dialogue, establishes a coming together, a correspondence between love and Resistance...*

Of course! Godard has always inscribed in his films, from one moment of history to the next, what he considered to be the points of resistance and creation, and more generally everything that in his eyes deserved to enter the composition of an image. What is essential for him, I think, is to allocate love between a strong, puritan conception of sexuality and a really amorous tension located more often in women, so that all men face the challenge of joining them or accepting their authority on this point. I have just worked with him on his next film, where I will possibly play the role of a philosopher-lecturer on a luxury cruise-ship, or perhaps I won't, because who knows what this artist will finally do with everything he has shot? I have admired close up his unique precision and his demanding stance. And it is love that is almost always at stake. Nevertheless, the melancholy that colours everything in Godard marks the difference between him and myself in terms of the connection between love and resistance. I feel incurably distant from that subjective colouring, even when love is at stake.

*Does the fascination for celebs, these new deities on a televised Olympus, stem, in your view, solely from political deception or is it evidence of an attraction for love stories that comes from the people's knowledge of the intensity of love?*

❧

There are two ways to read this phenomenon.
From a political perspective, one rapidly comes
to the conclusion that it is something fake. You
amuse and fascinate people with these stories
and that distracts them from what is really
important. In terms of politics, what interest can
there be in the fact that Carla succeeds Cécilia?
None at all, obviously. But you can also try to read
the publicity given to these events in a different
way by asking yourself: why does it work? It
must be because there is a generic interest in
love stories. It has always been the case that the
loves of the upper crust have been dramatised for
lower mortals. Why? There are also two possible
answers to that question. One can simply suggest
it has to do with love's universality: even Sarkozy
may be suffering as he desperately waits on a
text that never arrives. If you change the scales,
if you move from political truths to the truths
of love, your political enemy can end up being

like you, which isn't great, but it is reassuring. The love that can make a king suffer to an extent connects him with the serf. At that level, the serf is also a king. It is the romantic side of life: love is always in the air. But, there is a second interpretation: the apparent commonality in passion also shows that these guys, the king, the president, the Führer, the Father of the Peoples, aren't that special. They too can be cuckolded. So there is no fundamental reason to respect or fear them. We are back to politics, at least at its basic, subjective level.

As we said before, there are enemies in politics. So, we won't worry if they suffer in love. They'll never do us that honour! If we are at all politically aware, we must say that it is not our problem if Sarkozy's wife deceives him or not. But we should also say that we are interested in the visibility of love, at the level of a diffuse knowledge of love's virtues, a level that has

moreover been fortified by Christianity. This visibility is part of the boundless field where political
courage is fashioned from impure materials and
always starts from the position that enemies
have no supernatural significance and no transcendental power. To avoid getting bogged down
in Sarkozian mediocrity, I will give an example
of intense, sublime love from French history: one
that, at the time of the Fronde, linked the Queen
Regent Anne of Austria with that brilliant,
corrupt and devious politician, Mazarin. From
the point of view of the rioters, this love became
a terrible obstacle (the Regent will never leave
her man) and a vital ingredient in popular
rhetoric that represented Mazarin as a perverse
pig. I can think of no better way of saying that
only ambiguous connections exist between
politics and love, a kind of porous separation
or forbidden passage, that only the theatre can
properly account for. Comedy? Tragedy? Both.

ALAIN BADIOU

To love is to struggle, beyond solitude, with every-thing in the world that can animate existence. This world where I see for myself the fount of happiness my being with someone else brings. "I love you" becomes: in this world there is the fount you are for my life. In the water from this fount, I see our bliss, yours first. As in Mallarmé's poem, I see:

> *In the wave you become*
> *Your naked ecstasy.*